LIFE CYCLES

The
Beaver

Published by Raintree Steck-Vaughn Publishers, an imprint of Steck-Vaughn Company.

Acknowledgments
Project Editor: Pam Wells
Design Manager: Joyce Spicer
Editor: Sabrina Crewe
Designers: Ian Winton and Steve Prosser
Consultant: Michael Chinery
Illustrator: Andrew Pepworth
Electronic Cover Production: Alan Klemp
Additional Electronic Production: Scott Melcer
Photography credits on page 32

Planned and produced by The Creative Publishing Company

Library of Congress Cataloging-in-Publication Data
    Crewe, Sabrina
    The beaver / Sabrina Crewe ; [illustrator, Andrew Pepworth].
        p.   cm. — (Life cycles)
    Includes index.
    Summary: Follows two baby beavers, or kits, from birth to adulthood, describing their physical characteristics, behavior, and habitat.
    ISBN 0-8172-4376-3
    1. Beavers — Juvenile literature. 2. Beavers — Life cycles — Juvenile literature. [1. Beavers.] I. Pepworth, Andrew, ill. II. Title. III. Series: Crewe, Sabrina. Life cycles.
QL737.R632C74 1998
599.37′156 — dc21   96-40496
                                      CIP   AC

1 2 3 4 5 6 7 8 9 0 LB 01 00 99 98 97
Printed and bound in the United States of America.

Words explained in the glossary appear in **bold** the first time they are used in the text.

The
Beaver

Sabrina Crewe

RSVP

RAINTREE
STECK-VAUGHN
PUBLISHERS

The Steck-Vaughn Company

Austin, Texas

The beaver is getting ready.

In spring, the beaver makes a nest for its babies. The beaver's nest is inside a **lodge.** The lodge is home to a family of beavers.

The lodge is in a pond.

Beavers make their homes in ponds. They build their lodges with branches and twigs. The sticks are held together with mud. Inside the lodge, there is a room where the beavers live. They get in and out through tunnels under the water.

The beaver has two kits.

The beaver is **nursing** her new babies. Baby beavers are called kits. The kits feed on milk from their mother when they are small. When they are two weeks old, the other beavers in their family bring them plants to eat.

The kits stay close to their mother.

When the kits are a few weeks old, their mother takes them out of the lodge. They stay in the pond, swimming close to their mother. They are safer from **predators** if they stay in the middle of the pond. Otters sometimes **prey** on beaver kits while they swim in the pond.

The kit is a good swimmer.

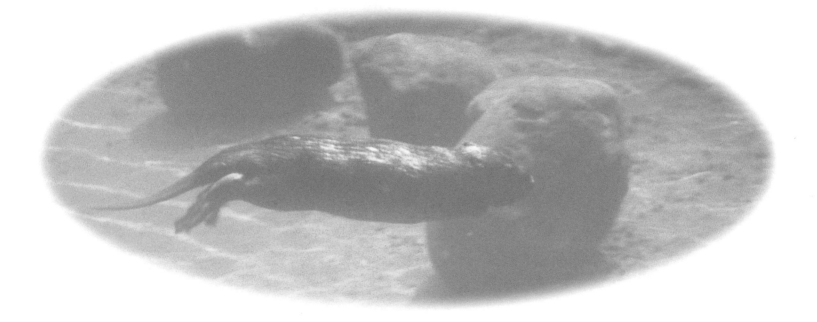

Kits can swim when they are just one day old. By the time they are two months old, they can swim in and out of the lodge by themselves. They use their webbed feet to paddle in the water. Their flat tails help them steer and balance.

The kit is eating twigs.

The mother beaver stops feeding milk to her kits when they are two months old. Now they find their food outside the lodge. At first they stay in the pond and eat small twigs from the family **food store**.

The young beavers grow fast.

As the kits get older, they leave the water to look for food. In their first year, they don't go far from the edge of the pond. In summer, there is plenty of food for beavers. They like to eat plants that grow in and around water. Beavers chew **bark** from tree branches, too.

The beaver oils its fur.

As beavers grow older, they start to make a special oil inside their bodies. They rub the oil on their fur to make it waterproof. Beavers also spread the oil on the ground around their ponds. The smell of the oil tells other animals that they are in the beavers' **territory**.

The beavers' pond has a dam.

The beavers have made their pond by building a **dam**. The dam is a wall of branches and logs across the stream. Behind the wall, the water builds up and spreads to make a pond.

The beaver is cutting a tree.

When the beaver is one year old, it starts to help with work around the family home. It helps to cut wood for fixing the lodge and the dam. The beaver uses its strong teeth to cut through trees.

The beaver takes the log to the pond.

When the tree has fallen, the beaver rolls it over the ground to the **canal**. The beaver digs canals from the trees to the edge of its pond. The canals fill with water. Then logs can float in the water all the way to the dam.

The beavers are fixing the dam.

The beavers build their dam with large logs.
Stones are used to hold the logs in place.
Then the beavers add mud and branches to
stop water from running through. They spend
a lot of time fixing their dams and lodges.

The coyote preys on beavers.

While the beavers are working on land, they are in danger. The coyote has come to hunt for food. Bears, mountain lions, and foxes also prey on beavers.

The beaver slaps its tail on the water.

The beaver senses that there is danger. Then it makes a loud noise by slapping its tail on the water. This signal tells other beavers that a predator has come to the pond. When they hear this, the beavers move into the deep water. They will be safe there.

The beaver is bringing a branch.

At the beginning of fall, the beavers cut small branches and twigs. They bring these to the pond. This way the beavers build up their food store for winter.

The beavers store food for the winter.

The beaver carries his branch down under the water. The beavers have made a store of food close to their lodge. When winter comes, there are no fresh plants growing at the pond. The beavers will eat bark from the branches they have stored in the pond.

The beavers are in the lodge.

In the winter, the beavers spend most of their time in the lodge. It is warmer inside, and they huddle together to keep warm. They can still get to their food store under the ice.

The beaver eats parts of willow trees.

In early spring, the beavers come out of the pond to look for food. They cut fresh twigs and look for new shoots growing on trees. Their favorite trees for food are aspen and willow trees.

The beaver has found a mate.

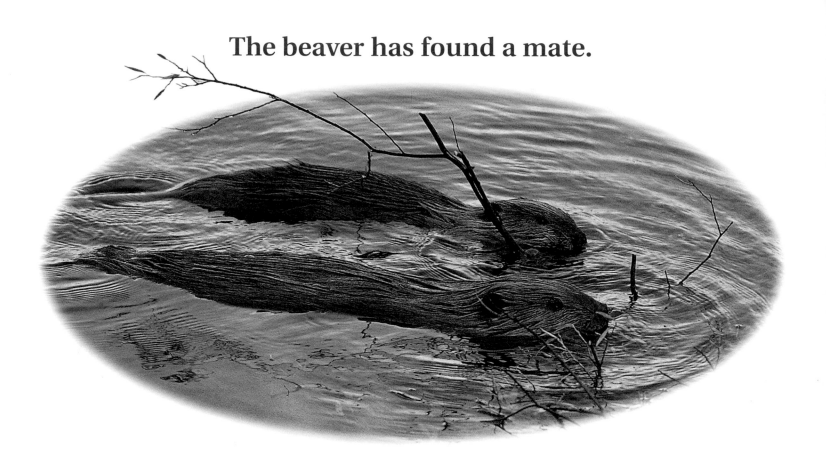

The young beavers leave their family home
when they are two years old. They swim
away in spring and look for other beavers
to mate with. The male beaver has found a
female beaver in a new territory.

The beaver makes a new home.

The beavers have made their own pond by building a dam. Now they are building a lodge. In winter, they will mate under the ice. A few months after the beavers mate, their babies will be born in the new lodge.

Beaver ponds are good for animals.

Beaver ponds are important places for many wild animals and **livestock**. Birds make their nests and find food near ponds. Large animals come to beaver ponds for water and food. Ponds make good homes for fish and plants. People can help many animals by letting beavers make ponds in wild places.

The Beaver Pond

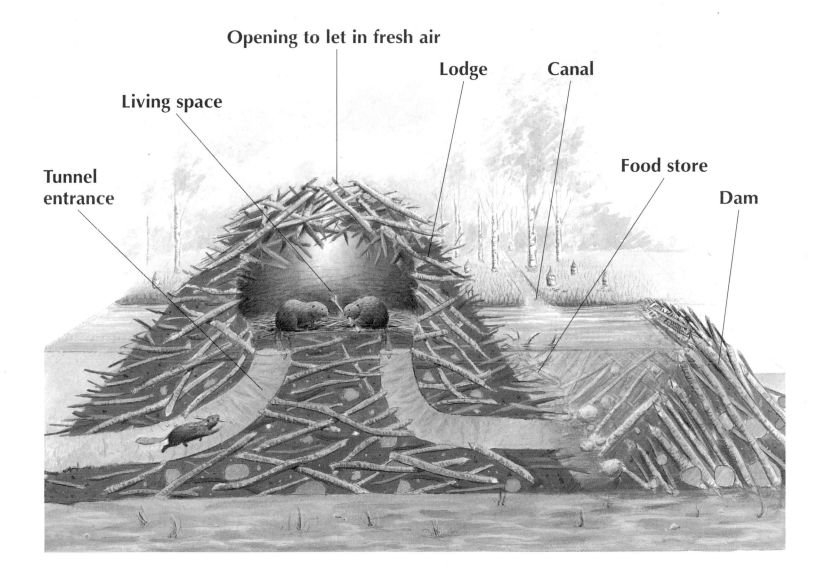

Opening to let in fresh air

Living space

Lodge

Canal

Tunnel entrance

Food store

Dam

Parts of a Beaver

Beavers belong to a group of **mammals** called **rodents**. Like other mammals, rodents are covered with fur and feed their young with milk. Rodents have four gnawing teeth at the front of their mouths.

Fur
Long, oily outer fur keeps water out
Soft underfur keeps body warm

Tail
Broad and flat for
paddling in water

Ears
Good hearing
Closed off when
underwater to
keep water out

Teeth
Strong and sharp
for gnawing wood
Keep growing as
they wear down

Front feet
Used for digging, holding,
and carrying

Back feet
Webbed for swimming
Claws for combing
and cleaning fur

Other mammals

The beaver in this book is the North American beaver. Beavers are the second largest rodents in the world, weighing up to 110 pounds (50 kg). Here are some other rodents and different kinds of small mammals.

Big-eared bat

Wood mouse

Flying squirrel

Yellow-pine chipmunk

Bobcat

European beaver

Snowshoe hare

Kit fox

Mole

29

Where the North American Beaver Lives

Alaska
(U.S.)

CANADA

UNITED
STATES

MEXICO

Areas where the
North American
beaver lives

Glossary

Bark The woody layer like a skin that covers trunks and branches of trees

Canal A channel that has been dug to carry things from one place to another by water

Dam A wall across a waterway that holds back the water

Food store The place where beavers keep a supply of food

Livestock Animals raised on farms, such as sheep and cattle

Lodge The den or home of a beaver

Mammal A kind of animal that usually has fur and feeds its young with milk

Nurse To feed young animals with mother's milk

Predator An animal that hunts and kills other animals for food

Prey To hunt or kill another animal for food

Rodent A type of mammal with four gnawing teeth at the front of its mouth

Territory An area of land that an animal defends as its own

Index

Photography credits